Copyright 2024 by Michael L. Clay. All Rights Reserved.
No part of this book may be reproduced or transmitted in any form or by any means, electronic or mechanical, including photocopying and recording, or by any information storage and retrieval system, without permission in writing from the author and publisher.

Printed in the United States of
America 2024 First Edition
10 9 8 7 6 5 4 3 2 1

Subject Index:
Clay, Michael L.
Title: I Found A Reason To Speak: Oneness For A Generation

Paperback ISBN: 979-8-9909584-0-1
Library of Congress Card Catalog Number: 2024915019
Written and photographed by Michael L. Clay
Cover Art: Khenya R. Clay
Made by Driven by Design Creative Agency LLC

www.dbdcreativeagency.com

To My Family:

Thank you for sharing your memories. Thank you for teaching me our families history from your POV. I'm learning more about me and building confidence as we travel together down the family tree. I have the baton to pass down our oral traditions for the next generation to see.

—Michael L. Clay

I FOUND A REASON TO SPEAK
ONENESS FOR A GENERATION

TABLE OF CONTENTS

1. A FATHER'S ACTION — 3
2. A MOTHER'S WORDS — 7
3. SEEDS — 11
4. NEVER EASY — 15
5. I FOUND A REASON TO SPEAK — 20
6. ON THE GARRY — 23
7. AUTONOMY — 27
8. FAMILY HISTORY — 31
9. YOUR STORY — 35

I just want to have a conversation.

My lens is more open, more focused, more driven with less opposition.

As a man, I want to continue to grow with a strong family bond. It's central to my world. It's in my minds eye.

Connection is Cultivated through Conversation.

These conversations are tough. We expect so much. We see the potential in our loved ones. Saying things like, "GET UP!" When its more to it. That is simply NOT ENOUGH. We see the ups and downs. We overthink or we don't think at all. We're blunt. We blurt out hurt. We interpret and disassociate. We assume and we don't ask questions.

I want something different.

Conversations gives us a chance to listen, to grow, to heal, to laugh, to cry, to build, to reflect, to empathize, to ask questions, to compromise, to understand life is nuanced.

It takes work to build a family.

Love is action, love is…words expressing an emotion, love are the seeds we conceive. No one said it would be easy, but you have a reason to speak your peace. Our ancestors chose the Garry and so did we. As we try, they cleaved. They spoke life into each other. It wasn't a fairy tale. They fought, but they knew how to come back to each other. Their bonds were tighter. Our words and actions must inflect the care we desire.

Words give me autonomy to move freely. My world is centered around my family. Here's some of our stories told through poetry by yours truly.

Chapter 1
A FATHER'S ACTION

The joyous days of growing his own
fruits and vegetables for his
wife and children in his home.
A father's dream is being able
to provide for his family.
His walk orchestrated my steps.
He gave me the tools to succeed.
Using his hands to lift as the
soil goes in between.
Bringing life with every touch
Just as God made you and me.

Chapter 2

A MOTHER'S WORDS

From the covering in her womb
to placing me in a bassinet;
wrapping me in that cocoon.
Showing me how to guard against
those who wound.
She fed me words of wisdom
till there was no more room and
less insecurities to roam.
My mother said,
"Don't believe the hype."
"They don't know me so,
it shouldn't cause you to fight."

Chapter 3
SEEDS

Words are seeds that take root.
The etymology.
The land is your history and ancestry.
Weathered, fertile or brittle?
What did my family sow into me
becoming genetically a part of me?

That root becomes your speech.
Some grow up straight.
Others... Well, we burrow deep.

Each plant has a life expectancy;
a circuitry.
The inner workings
showing itself outwardly.

On one hand,
**grabbing nutrients native
to my environment**.
Water and illuminating sunlight
refreshing my body.
Or with two hands,
grabbing nutrients from
everything around me.
Uprooting, changing my trajectory.

It all depends on your conditioning.
With each day we are learning,
growing, building and destroying.
All to become stronger
in this life…we call home.

From the Niger to Ancient Nagas
Knowledge.
Separated and still
saying the same things.
Our language almost identical
using logos to speak.
Mdw Ntr.
Rest in peace Jacob Carruthers.
It's Never Easy. Divine speech.
The hieroglyphs with other studies
is where I would find other
Messiahs before He.
The definition of deity.
Horus and Isis; the bisexual beings.
That's a reference to duality.
Yin & Yang; the XI people.
Not just sexuality.
We must come together. **Oneness.**
Both of us. It's you and me.

Division has never carried us
through our transgressions and iniquities.
The Black Image in Antiquity.
Rest in Peace Runoko Rashidi.
It's Never Easy.
We are beautiful, royal and divine.
It is written in our history.
We were here thousands of years
populating the earth. Olmec head.
The African Presence in Ancient America
They Came Before Columbus.
Rest in Peace Ivan Van Sertima.
It's Never Easy.
Amarucan aborigines
still the same kin to me,
not Amerigo Vespucci.

A part of your family
has documented history.
The other is a mission.
Mines Natchez Nation vicinity
where I find similarities
to both sides of my family through history.
One side from the West Indies
and the other from Mississippi.
Could it be I'm on a trail to find
the missing links to our identities?
Possibly a land mass for us through a treaty.
Tracing Your Family's Genealogical
History by Records, Dane Calloway.
My dad told me Natchez currently
is rural and ripe with KKK.
Home of Elvis Presley.
Never said it would be easy...

Chapter 5

I FOUND A REASON TO SPEAK

I've always been behind the camera
both in photography and filmmaking.
Capturing moments of people
telling their stories, their history,
and our identities both from
the past and in the present.
But there was one interview
that stuck out that made me
see differently.
Mr. Tyrone Gaskins
from the Trenton community.
He uttered these words,
**"You must become an expert
in your issue of advocacy."**

For me, most times
I only saw the imagery.
I mean I'm a part of it.
It's my bread and butter.
But no one really spoke directly;
from a direct approach of law.

They would just skim right past it.
Just scratching the surface
as if it really didn't matter.
We are called law abiding citizens,
so why don't I know the law?

I think I found my calling,
well at least a part of it.
It is my soliloquy to move forward.
To pass on information.
To teach the willing.
This is what grounds me.
It is sewn into my being.
Walking around from behind
to in front of the camera.
It is my duty!

I FOUND A REASON TO SPEAK!

Chapter 6
ON THE GARRY

I was reading how the Gullah Geechie
passed down their history
orally through storytelling.
Now we practicing on the Garry.
To hear the stories from way back when.
The generations sitting there listening.
Bringing back them oral traditions.

Its a once in a lifetime opportunity.

We traveling from state to state.
So sit back and enjoy the ride.
As we go down all the 95s
to Lloyd Gaddis farm where the
tale begins on I-55.

My Aunt Rosie Lee spoke to me
as we breezing through traffic.
She began speaking on the
meanings of past tense.
Like, "Mike, you ever heard of
'On the Garry?'"

We all do it. It's a daily occurrence.
Conversing on the porch,
replicating on the walk and the talk.
The memories shared between family.
It's groomed from our thoughts.

Like remember when
Willie stalled out on praying.
Everyone closed their eyes
sitting there waiting. I mean he humming,
but I don't hear nothing.
I opened my eyes
to see him crawling away.
Now ain't that something.
Man we blessed!

Everyone don't get a chance like this.
To speak to those who lived it.
They're planting the seeds in me to share
with my nephews and nieces.
To pick up the pieces right where they left off.
Aunt Ollie B said,
"It took him to come from New Jersey
to see our families
beginnings still standing."

Welcome to the McCray family...

ON THE GARRY!

Chapter 7
AUTONOMY

For years I've been trying to
understand ME in this world and as I've gotten
older, a better listener and observer,
I've realized in order to become a masterpiece
You must follow some rules:

One.

Reflecting back from a fractured mirror
remembering all the ideas presented
Don't match with my center.
Through each endeavor
I'm offered an opportunity to choose
My own destiny.

Starting from a litany of introspective identities
pushing forward present day
while simultaneously pulling past dismays
As Restitution…to keep me company.
We're just looking for an opportunity.
Mines…is right in front of me.

I know that each and every iterative action
I take envelops my experience.
I'm far removed from
YOUR idea of a delinquent.

I have an intrapersonal experience
delineated from a composite etched.
God fearing? Yes!
Most definitely.
But my ideas aren't your ideas
and your ideas, I don't covet.

Same subject. Different path.
I've accepted your judgement and
I've moved wayyyyy past that.
Accepting the movements of
Creating and becoming
My very own masterpiece.

AUTONOMY

Chapter 8
FAMILY HISTORY

Begin your family history journey by asking the oldest living members this question: **"What's your earliest memory?"** When I did that all my Great Aunts & Uncles, my grandmother and her children began sharing their stories.

I wish I would have known early on the importance of connecting via first hand accounts with my family and our history. It has put perspective into the books I've read by giving me real life application. I have better insight on specific regions and the impact it had on my family from generation to generation. It has built my confidence in so many ways with the added fortunate opportunity to still ask questions. *Please do not let any chapter close, else you'll get second and third hand narratives instead of the primary resource.*

I've left some lines for you to begin writing down your stories. If you need further guidance, I've also attached a story starter.

1. Write a poem or journal about the family stories you've gathered.

_____
_____
_____
_____
_____
_____
_____
_____
_____
_____
_____
_____

FAMILY HISTORY

FAMILY HISTORY

Chapter 9

YOUR STORY

1. Write a poem or journal about the impact those stories have placed on your life.

YOUR STORY

Definitions

Autonomy - The power or right of self-government; the doctrine that the human will carries its guiding principle within itself; law.

Delineated - Drawn; marked with lines exhibiting the form or figure; sketched, designed, painted, described.

Etymology - The investigation of the origin or derivation and the original signification of words; the science that treats of the origin and history of words; the part of grammar relating to inflection.

Interpersonal - being, relating to, or involving relations between persons.

Intrapersonal - Occurring within the individual mind or self.

Introspective - To see within.

Iterative - Repetition; repeating.

Oneness - Singular; unity.

Restitution - The act of returning or restoring to a person some thing or right of which he has been unjustly deprived.

Soliloquy - A talking to one's self; a talking or discourse of a person alone, or not addressed to another person, even when others are present.

From the 1828 Noah Webster's American Dictionary of the English Language, 1898 Chambers's English Dictionary & Merriam-Webster.com

About the Author

Michael L. Clay is a husband, uncle, son, brother, CEO, Multimedia Visual Storyteller, Lifestyle Photographer, teaching artist and creative writer.

As a conduit in communication, his desire is to infuse the freedom of oral storytelling tradition with a focus on interpersonal dialogue amongst families. Through the writings and visuals he shares, Michael yearns to invoke a larger conversation centered around understanding one's race[1]. Michael uses visual aesthetics to illuminate and interrogate words' root, context and subject matter to tell a vivid and a more cohesive point of view.

Whether its his students learning how to write creatively during his programs, documenting the history of those around him or capturing his own family stories, Michael seeks to discover the joy, humanity and all else in between as they redefine their autonomy.

In 2020, Michael developed his very own gentle action in the marketplace; a creative writing board game called Story Driven. Story Driven is a fun, interactive enrichment learning and assessment tool that helps its players become the writers they never thought they could be. The board game caters to its players writing level while simultaneously aiding them as they grow as writers. It's an outlet for its players to express themselves through several writing methods. One story can be told multiple ways leaving no room for redundancy and opens the door to exploration.

[1] *Race - lineage of a family; a generation; a family of descendants; common ancestry. 1828 Noah Webster: American Dictionary of the English Language & the Chambers English Dictionary*

SERIES COMING SOON

Story Driven
UNLOCKING WRITER'S BLOCK

#1 CREATIVE WRITING BOARD GAME TO UNLOCK WRITER'S BLOCK

Freeing Generations from Writer's Block!

Alleviates writing anxiety.

The starter kit to creative writing.

Creative writing through your own lens.

An enrichment learning tool for professionals.

Helps its players think outside the box. (ELA, Literacy & SEL)

Develop future script writers.

Child and parent engagement.

Bringing families together to share stories.

Fun for the entire family.

DBDCREATIVEAGENCY.COM

Made in the USA
Middletown, DE
26 November 2024